W<small>E</small>,

We, Day by Day

Jin Eun-young

Translated by
Daniel Parker & YoungShil Ji

WHITE PINE PRESS / BUFFALO, NEW YORK

White Pine Press
P.O. Box 236
Buffalo, New York 14201
www.whitepine.org

Publication of this book was made possible, in part, by grants from the
Literature Translation Institute of Korea.

Cover art: .*Flower Rain in Water Village* by Simon Xianwen Zeng. Private
collection. Used by permission of the artist.

First Edition

Korean Voices Series, Volume 25

ISBN: 978-1-945680-11-3

Library of Congress Control Number: 2017946293

Printed and bound in the United States of America.

We, Day by Day

Contents

3. Literary Life

Translators' Introduction

In his introductory note for *The Lion's Tail and Eyes*, Robert Bly referred to Eugenio Montale's statement that "If the purpose of poetry lay in making oneself understood, there would be no purpose in writing it." Bly later adds, "The poem expresses what we are just beginning to think, thoughts we have not yet thought. The poem must catch these thoughts alive, holding them in language that is also alive, flexible and animal-like as they."

In this book, noted South Korean philosopher-poet Jin Eun-young continues her experimental arrangements of words that result in elusive or even incoherent images. These images, however challenging, are never careless or dull. She has stated her desire to use her imagery to present new sensual experiences to herself as well as her readers, preferring to stimulate the senses instead of communicating meaning. She doesn't reject communication, she says, but she rejects "language that can be used only for communication."

Jin's poems are very readable and compelling, but always challenging for the reader seeking complete comprehension. This fits well with Jin's overall personality. Although critics have labeled her as "courageous" for her poetry, literary criticism, and social activism, she describes herself as someone who feels threatened by brightness, and who prefers the safety of shadows and darkness. Many poems in this collection present dramatic scenes of night, because she feels nights are for concealment. However, she adds, night does not erase flaws or failures; in fact, the senses become more delicate — so new things are revealed inside that which is hidden.

The overall book is formed by a mixture of "reserved and divided voices of poetic speech that hasn't been yet systematized, denying the lyrical identity of '90s poems," according to literary critic Lee Gwang-ho. Thus, her poetry has shades of Choi Seung-ja's influence, but the gap between Jin's intense, descriptive consciousness and her concise expressions shine in their own light.

As noted literary critic Hahm Don-kyoon notes, Jin is "becoming one of the rare poets who remain loyal to their poetic beliefs."

In her youth, Jin felt cheerful while reading the works of Friedrich Nietzsche. She stated that since his poor health did not prevent deep thinking and sharp, honest writing, it gave her courage to face her own health problems.

She went on to earn a Ph.D. in Western Philosophy from prestigious Ehwa Women's University and has published three books of philosophy, along with three books of poetry. Her writing has also been published in several anthologies and collaborative works.

The paradoxes and sensual fragments found in her poems reflect the attitude of a poet who recognizes the world as Spinoza stated: "I have labored carefully, not to mock, lament, or execrate, but to understand human actions."

Jin often declines to show us the entire image or even to provide context for its meaning, but, as Bly noted about the imagery of The Lion's Tail and Eyes, "We have to understand that the rest of the lion is there."

—YoungShil Ji and Daniel T. Parker

Foreword

To our poet, Choi Seung-ja

When I was in college,
in the subway commuting
between home and school,
I always used to imagine you.
If you were sitting on this subway,
among these many people,
would I recognize you?

Jin Eun-young
—August 2008

I.
Melancholia

Today we shall complete his melancholia —
Maybe this is what things I met have said;
things like the darkness of the shop,
the window where azaleas dream in confusion.

— Boris Pasternak

Beautiful

If you were beautiful today
you'd be like a shining hairpin in a dead woman's hair,
like a picture that catches the blind man's eye,
like kids in muslin pajamas, chattering
as they pass through fog, drunk on the cherries' scent.
You'd be like the salty taste of the giraffe's long neck in the savanna
during the rainy season and

you'd dissolve slowly and be absorbed by a wide red cloth—
dehydrated white crystals
sprinkled like sand on decaying gills.
Today

if you are beautiful
it's like a hazy green funnel of seaweed stench
that rises and drifts across a landfill

The Snow Queen

Things stolen from her
fit all
objects wrapped in white bearskin.
Swollen barley seeds germinate;
a garbage truck, a red mailbox, houses float.

Cars have stopped
Scrapped tires, dark
as my lover's nipples, roll

On such an early morning, people
rise like daggers
to chase
the killer who left the burgundy skin

White hairs carried on wind escape into the air.

Melancholia

He painted me as sweetly as
ice cream dropped on hot asphalt.
I begin to melt, never
touching the tip of a tender tongue.

He always feels sad because of me.
He painted me on a sandy desert
and now remembers that he painted a fish.
He summons the desert wind
and erases me.

He's a real optimist.
He believes I went to the sea.

The Dot

Descartes' dot,
the dot trapped in a closed curve,
the dot that doesn't fill the other side of a written page.
No matter how many are gathered,
there's only one dot.

The dot on the bridge of your nose,
like the talon of a white owl soaring into white sky
gripping a sheepskin pouch full of mint leaves.

The languid dot that I love.
Like a black peppercorn star adrift on the nose of the cosmos,
provoking a mild sneeze,
your face, a white fig composed in mysterious geometry

A Gypsy's Time

A woman in a black pointed hat hated lessons.
Using a knife, she scraped pure white languor from kids' tongues
and took them into shade where the fragrance of plums flowed down.

She poured liquor into our small ears:
stories like drinking wine for the first time.
She pulled knife-edged time from a purple leather pouch.

Empty,
she slammed down the bottle she was drinking from.
Under the night sky, we lay with her on the sand.
Black loaches flopped, pricked by twinkling shards of glass.

On an even darker day,
she flowed into boys' bodies
like moonlight flowing down
through only one narrow window
in a dark hallway.

What else could she steal?
With no light and extremely cold air,

she wrapped kids' white necks in a long scarf glittering
like the Milky Way,
round and round,
then left on a black train.

Danger: stand behind the line.
She knocked down the platform sign.
Leaning far out of the window, she gave her final farewell

Chewing jelly beans blue as the sky,
we sat on a floral-patterned sofa abloom with a smoky scent
and read aloud the postcards she sent.

Kids, as your city flattens,
as it flattens like a dipping dish of sticky yellow oil,
please sink it
in the oak wash bowl I gave you,

or, *I have enclosed a catalogue of the city I just created.*

May her hat tear the night air's tender tongue
and soar like a star.

Little kids practiced lopsided letters in their tablets
and kids a little bit older shooed birds out of the zodiac.

In the continuing cold,
we shook
like the tambourine she left behind

There ——

they enter quickly despite my persistent pushing
on the revolving door of consciousness, a scent wafting
        from your rented house,
its darkened windows.
Rain scatters transparent fishhooks
through ashy gray branches.
My rubber boots hang upside down.
There — things fall from my vest's turned-out pocket:
bits of yarn tangled in lint, lumps of yellow paper.
There — black rain blurs
and stains crumpled blank space.
There — for so long hospitable to sorrow.
There — pure starched-white disillusionment of faded hostility
Ah there – miscellaneous thoughts about a certain body
I touched
I slowly climb to the top of a dark tower,
wet stars mingling with the smell of rotting melon.
I stretch my arms down to reach the dry, empty floor
and my pale fingers sway, there —
there —

I Want to Know Why:

Nights, like the backs of Tarot cards, are arrayed in a sequence; dahlia petals twirl on the surface of water. *Why?* There is no wall but I keep banging on the door. The hot juice of apple pie runs down, down my neck. Unused light bulbs are broken in glass factories. *Why?* Washed clothes take so long to dry. A blue bird sings and flies up (*I love you* —) to autumn skies above a black cherry tree. And, *why on earth* I write poems. Why ashes are soft after paper is burnt.

Jumbled Stories

"Sleep or smoke as you will; be silent, be somber."
I like quotations that have lost their sources,
a grey brick fallen from a hard rampart,
my mouth inflamed by
spicy ginger cookies,
and huge feet

From the ankles of a steel trestle
broken, swaying and turning red with rust,
from thatched roofs rotting,
through a wild ox's wet hair,
from distant fields,
a sweet, warm wind blows

I like using my fingers,
the difficulty of saying no,
all drafts.
I like clumsy gestures,
move-in days.
I like
the tranquility of a dead person's casually arranged feet,
grassy grave mounds above those feet—
like green breasts collected in a cemetery,
a living person's coughing, and the nipple of despair he suckles.
But the time when honey and snow blends together,

the blue time, like ice running down
your face, neck,
back, I like
the burnt flavor of the last herring
we grilled together
in burnt ashes.

Ra-Ra-Rapunzel

He loves stray cats and shadows. A white dove flies up from the coffin where he lies. I grow lettuce in a vast open field and live in a tall tower that rises unexpectedly among tender green leaves. The evening bell of an old Catholic cathedral peals across the field, and his voice is heard nearby. *No stairs, nor door; young lady, please let your long fair hair down through the narrow window.*

Women who keep their hair long
are played like music for a very long time ...

Already this is the eighth time he's pulled my hair to climb up and chop off my head. He tosses it out the window and it bounces like a deflating ball ... I cry *Hello, meow-meow, I'm also a cat.* Today I'm reborn into my ninth life. Hundreds of snails. I alone run in a black canvas where no one is painted.

Torn lettuce leaves rise on the wind and slap my face.

Blue Shirt

He's been falling for a while
then gets caught in the air

The branch is frail and delicate. Soon she will break.
Together or separately,
caressing the transparent and long waist of the fall,

both of his freed arms stir
the wound in the wide flank that gapes
like green rose petals

down
       down

Rules of Love

You caress my nape
with fingers that rubbed thyme's small petals yesterday.
I watch you sleep
lest unfamiliar animals dig up
our graves, newly built in soft sand.
Warm pebbles on the beach, seaweed,
thrusting our white toes
deep against seashell's pink tongues,
we walk in the world's navel.

And we hold on to each other's existence
like a boxer dripping yellow sweat in the empty gym on Wednesday
hugs the punching bag as it returns, then sinks to the floor alone.

A Wanderer

After such a long walk,
the insides of his boots
are soaked like bloodied cotton balls.

Sitting on discarded tires in an empty lot,
little kids wave sparklers over their blackened knee.s
Hens on the tin roof lay white eggs
that roll down to the edge of the eaves.

He slowly passes
along the frontier connected by women's
twisted blue stockings,
dripping water
from the barrack's old fraying clothesline

The black forest
blocks airborne answers from cities
with a flash of dreamers' dark green shields.

Train wheels bear down
on railroad ties, the amputated arms of beeches.
Leaves fly up and shatter
then descend silently,
cross the monorail,
hover among the sound
of his murmuring:
What will be picked up by those two long
silver chopsticks?

Blades of gray grass
stuck like hair in a drain on the side of a stream
that flows, barely audible.

Stepping-stones. In early December, in soaked socks,
jumping
from this to that star,
from one to another girl,
from permanent green to permanent gray.

Answer me:
Whose lover am I?
he asks his frozen feet
for the last time

Wind Song

Yes, shaking twigs, I tried to drop blackberries
into a milk pail.
I tried polishing the noses of brown leather shoes
which shone like crescent moons until dulled by dust.

Yes, I saw white clouds, tender dough of the sky, stiffening.
Charred black bread crumbled and fell on people's heads.

Yes, I heard a poem with burgundy wings fly away
after perching briefly on a dead branch.
The soul from my ear mixed with ash and wandered the street.

Yes, I hung around with fire.
Chairs couldn't accept my thick gray butt
so they blazed fiercely.

When You Were a Boy

you liked an imprisoned maiden, a small portal, a magic yoyo,
apple vinegar, fake names of several colors,
rafts broken apart by even slightly sad songs.
Running with eyes closed down wooden stairs
how beautiful the creaking.

You hated the evil Belt Satan, oil wars, excuses.
Ice stars shivered on a yellow lambswool blanket,
well-worn coins fell into a broken fountain
sounding like water drops.

When you were a boy
I wished to eat the plums you picked,
when I had no breasts, heavy as stones, under my black polka dot dress.

When a girl loved a girl,
when a boy loved a boy

                              when you held a strange sparkler
between thumb and forefinger,
burning huge parentheses on the yellow test paper,
wanting to paint houses red,
wearing underwear caught by fire
tight against the cold skin of the war and passing summer.

Shoe Seller's Song

I didn't come to find a cause; instead, I came to create a cause
— Hera-Xanthippe, 387 B.C.
(from a memo blown away on the evening wind)

You don't know how beautiful were the slippers you dropped in such haste.
Tonight the bell rings again and I go around picking up slippers you lost
You don't know why you laughed.

I've come to inform you
that tonight I'm endlessly picking up slippers
to make shoes for a weird guy with huge feet

You can take it all:
my wet hands, my drunken time, my voice.

You like clocks busy with broken hours; you
open the smoothly-moving Big Ben
and throw down a small screw inside it.

We politely hid the *telos* of revolution above brilliant clouds.
So, just as we pass

we throw slippers into the glass forest
for the cuckoos' funny cries—
5:25, 5:26, 5:27—
for the wet red feathers of birds that sing without rest.

Bombs don't explode on time.
Clouds scatter everyday.

Here comes a poor glass seller.
Anyway, I loved you,
loved the only white foot,
like a memory that never wore a wristwatch

Extinction

On a Sunday when I ride to the zoo
in a red car,

like a bird sitting on a car horn,

      the sky is a blue partition
      separating us from the mysterious higher realm.

Soon songs will fly
from the scene on faded wings;
in a dead-end alley
the agile and the
increasingly slow will disappear

An august tree with a growing green tumor:
long death, like a snake climbing to constrict it.
                    Across the street,
like a piano with a broken leg,
the world is tilting.

      Darkness.
Light in the window sways like a lemon.

I've never told truths.
They write themselves and fill a white notebook as darkness falls.

We, Day by Day

With cherries stuffed
in the pockets of our white shirts
we fall day by day

Green tomatoes hurled high
ripen to red in the 5 p.m. air
and ooze down

We consider at great length
in order to say the wrong things,
shake darkness inside an ebony chest that has no key

Our four seasons
a sour quartered orange.

Drawing deep breaths, fragrances explode from pipes,
we, day by day.

2.

Songs of Crazy Love

I am too hot and scorched with my own thought:
often is it ready to take away my breath.
Then have I to go into the open air,
and away from all dusty rooms

— Friedrich Nietzsche
Thus Spake Zarethustra

Mephisto Waltz

When scarlet sage bloomed
in a coffin that had lost its cover and corpse,
and the night stared with stunned eyebrows
at ivy growing over tombstones,
when anxieties clustered
like grapes on the broken cross of my shoulder-blade,

something was trapped in the empty cistern of my heart.
If only it could swim in remembered ripples of dark blood;
if forgotten secrets could again plunge into my body;
if I were caught in the fragile hues of porcelain;
if I were dancing wildly on a Persian carpet.

Every pore stopped up by sadness,
the odorless street's lavender petals trampled by tires,
the moon's lips faded as ancient money, ancient plague.

That night when rotting onions rolled
from the torn sack of darkness,

before I became ice melting in the alcohol you drink,
before the flaming violin burned the white birch forest,
he came,

a blue cricket chirping in my dead ears

Modification

Scenery of scarlet chairs,
women's names like clouds and gemstones.
The street drags the sound of evening bells and cars
into the mashed light-green of boiled peas.

Poetry—groping in the darkness.
Closing my eyes so I can grope

Tender tongues of hungry dogs lick my fingers; the thick fragrance of the
skin of a lemon that has been sucked dry; slightly sad and funny feelings;
written symbols; the bumpy plaster wall my palms touch; the moon a huge
lens! More than that, the cold wound of my forehead touching it and the
bitter taste of sand

The magic square totals zero when added up, the same as the number of
senses I count in the wind blowing through the empty square

In the Middle of the Night

A cat is a reason for a roof.
Holding a passing cat, the roof gushed a red cry.
The velvety black tail
caressed the roof for a long, long time

I dumped the dead roses; memory shivered, red,
flowed down the drain with the water from the jar.
Roses are a reason for a jar.

White feet walked out of big black boots
and disappeared somewhere in the middle of the night.
I embraced the empty jar with all my might.
I was broken.

Youth #3

Let us, since all
passes, pass
I shall look back only too often
                              — Apollinaire
                                    "Hunting Horns"

Iron gates were most beautiful with the first coat of orange,
no matter whether exits or entrances

A red glass tulip bloomed
among flying stones.

Soft heels of dreams
trampled the wounded forehead.

I remember

two transparent icebergs; your cleavage,
where a snowstorm and mint fragrance blustered,
where I ran to bury my burning face.

Anthology

I have five poets
The first one is sick
All night long,
like a brightly-lit floor in an abandoned black building,
his pain glitters
in the corner where the blind hours strike

The second one is brave.
He moves from the polarity of his youth,
where glass petals shattered,
toward a hooded cobra, rusty gun muzzles,
the frontier looming like a coniferous forest
March!
Soon you will die
is written on a dried halibut.
      Chewing the delicious letters,
drooling watery saliva,
he starts out again
—dear God, his jaw breaks

Thus
in a night slain and blanched by midnight sun,
the third poet masquerades as a doctor.
I'm a dark cathedral with no visitors!
he shouts.
He likes St. Peter, whose shadow healed the sick.

My fourth poet is a genius.
He never sings.
Face down on the floor,
he dreams of endless kisses.
In a dream within a dream, his teeth hold
the nipple of a huge, soft balloon,
a star inflated by his warm breath.

The last one
is bullshit.
Another five live in his cracked voice;
each one owns five birds
that spit green spit, *ptui-ptui*
their feathers incubate images.

Beyond ripped-out trees
onto the vibrating excavator
ashy feathers
                   of various colors
                                    swaying
                                             falling

The last one is bullshit
The world begins unaccustomed rotations
on the axis of one of his clumsy lines.

I Am

too much boiled spinach, a lollipop tossed away while still being licked, a house wrapped round and round with a tapeworm, broken scissors, a gas station that sells watered-down gasoline, fish scales scattered on the chopping board, a compass with an ever-spinning needle, a thief of rotting fruit, sleep that never comes, a wet hand thrust inside a sack of flour, a one-legged man's broken crutch, the nipple of a yellow balloon that was over-inflated and burst when certain lips touched.

That Day — I

That day — I touched poetry's lips for the first time.
That day — I rained down like stars.
That day — I walked into the bright dark light,
sweeping my hair back.

That day — I saw a lizard for the first time,
toddling to grab its blue tail.
That day — I laughed, showing white teeth for the first time.
That day — I spun with arms outstretched
in the whirling warm sand.

That day — I ran into the road.
That day — I tossed hundreds of pieces of paper into the sky.
You watched me, hiding behind
a curtain's vertical blue stripes.
That day, you disappeared, leaving only the blue tail in my hands

Who drummed an empty tin can in the summer yard?
Whose dazzlingly white elbows were exposed by short sleeves?
Who shouted, *Me, it's me,* behind the thick wall?
That day, when you were gone,

all the sand in the hourglass flowed down and I turned it over.

Artificial Lake

The odor of dead plants and animals
is absorbed in my face.
Even in slight sunshine
sorrow like green plankton
covers me.

Summer Snow

Truths are illusions about which one has forgotten
that this is what they are; metaphors which are worn out
and without sensuous power.
—Nietzsche

Adam asks,
What's your name?
Hair beautifully matted with hide glue—
wind blowing through short black grass.

Adam. The first city
is under the frozen lake.
A freezing fish
eats water bubbling from the gray wall.
What's the name of that fish?

Fins aflame, I say,
I'm a poet.
Don't call me by a different name.
I don't want to hear it.
I swing my burnt fins.

From the mirrored forest
a female apple seller
brings two red breasts on a platter.

Adam, taking a big bite, asks
What's your name?

I'm Herod, I'm John's severed head,
I'm the father to all the sons I killed.

There is no metaphor,
just blue ice
melted inside a warm hole.

Adam, what's my name?
It's grape urine flowing out of holes
in oak barrels piled
under the stairs of the black moon,
the basement we left a long time ago.

It's
the disappearing blue ice mirror,
burnt skin, snowflakes descending to the river floor,

Under the lake
is the first city;
the passing fish eating blizzard snow;
burnt names

The blue-black surface is freezing, shaping a mosiac wave.

Water

resting in the dark, waiting for someone,
shivering for a moment,
unknown things flow to me and become known,
simply shivering for a moment,
the unchanging flow of water,
waiting for someone in the water,
water becoming transparent, momentarily reflecting me,
the unchanging color of water
until once-blue things flow to me and become blue.

(When I feel so cold and bored with this
shall I imagine there's a leak in me?)

unknown things flowing to me, soaking in little by little,
stiff serifs inside me soaking, gradually softening,
gradually swelling,
a sleep relaxing into asleep,
the house growing large as a house, a sea becoming deep as the sea,
unknown things flowing to me,
flowing, going, dissolving my interior red paint,
water hue making me warm for a moment,

in these reveries, forgetting for a moment, water.

One Day

The sea was an immense emerald teardrop, then entirely absorbed in a single grain of sand. I laughed, cutting a white onion. You chewed marmalade, tossing fireworks carelessly. Cold baseballs rolled around on the playground. On the horizon, birds shrieked as they crashed through the blue.

You gifted a white whale with your ear.

You had to drink again today, until the soft bed of the sky was completely exposed.

A conch shell was half-buried in muddy clouds; you had to find a lost earring.

A sweet sun rose above an orange bay. Burgundy leaves on roofs along the coastline's long tongue became luxuriant. My mind was a dust-bunny clinging to a broom. I was a woman who perhaps resembled a walnut tree. I stretched out my arms. Many heavy walnuts hung. They swayed like the broken ropes of playground swings. *The age when everything brilliantly matched has gone,* you shouted. All through the clanging iron afternoon, you searched for the afternoon that was absent. The sunshine was a baseball game in the bottom of the ninth. It absorbed everything. Like a closer with bases loaded, I was not lonely. Beneath the shop's showcase, the nutcracker soldier's shattered jawbones clattered on the dry floor.

To a Critic

A long train, a long black train.
You board,

opening the window, ask,
Where am I? Where am I?

You memorize names of passing towns, alphabets of several countries,
cite the differences between Welsh and Scottish pronunciation,
report the exact length and width of the tunnel the train just passed
through.

I'm your boss, but today's your day off.

Here's your assignment:
Ride the names of the towns, perhaps as long as tapeworms or as aromatic
as kudzu. Be sure to feel the whoosh of something whooshing through the
crotch of your thin pants. Before you realize it, inhale darkness that
clutches your lungs like tentacles. Swallow the unchewed-noodle slashes of
light.

Get off. Take a nap. You must be a little tired
although tickled by foxtails beside the dark tracks.
. . .*zzz*. . .

To help you earn a ride on my train,
I gently, all night long . . .
drip, drop by drop, random sounds floating through my body
in the hardened dough of darkness.

To Me

Questions, little by little
hesitantly swell like a girl's white breasts.

Nothing happens.
Goodbye, sad hazy afternoon.
Goodbye, beautiful openings in brass instruments.
Goodbye, black covers of closed books.

Goodbye, flawless crusts of hot bread.
Senses are birthed in cracks
like a turtle shell in a bonfire.

Burn the hardback book,
predict something,
love contingency.

Inside the book,
the extinguished flame.
Forget what's on the stove.

The die is cast.
Words are broader than their meanings — in the lush grassy field
numbers lie hidden. Surround the forest with the scent of sulfur
and be an inventor of shuddering.

Give me the final poem.
The topic is aesthetically tired but it moves my heart
from *there* to *here.*

This poet gets as wet as a shaken bowl of water.
This person always returns in ruin.
This person likes long sky feathers spreading beyond broken walls.
Blue feathers that slowly descend
to jasmine landmines, a battered tank of rambling roses

to the holes in women's and children's faces.
Let your face express water
that will fill the broken bathtub.

Failed poets.
Failed revolutions.
Firework
smoke reeks from pink plastic.

Fail again fail better.
Fireworks in water.

Before the Rooster Crows

Birds soar through the hole pierced in my back,
bitter smell of dry mugwort spreads across the cold floor.
I gnaw at conjunctions with my back teeth,
nostalgic for the oven inside the apple.
Please say you don't know me.
Dawn is already coming,
dawn so blue in heavy fog
that I cannot ponder
profound meanings,
warm bread, or muddy futures that harden easily.

A Day When I'm Sick and Alone

This afternoon, the fragrance of drying hay climbs the stairs.
Waiting for you, I polished
all the black cherries hanging between the leaves.
Paper stars on my door sway in the wind, so
don't throw the door open; the empty pharmacy bags will blow away.
The stashed pills are meant for the palms of lost kids;
their siblings, who may never find their way.

Then I will say only to the birch woods and birds, to you:

I have six moles on my body.
Today I created a fruit knife,
had a long talk with pain,
who said it wasn't interested in murder
but must be maniacally addicted to beautiful stabs.
And I,
like orange inside black,
am somehow gradually fading.

What does this disease smell like?
I've heard a plague smells like a ripe apple, measles
like newly-plucked feathers.

What if you suddenly waken between green and red,
between three drops of honey on your forefinger
and a nest of fierce wasps.
In a field of jittery asparagus instead of gaudy ornaments
on plates?

Tonight what disease should you suffer from? What poetry?

I have only six moles on my body.
Night's fingers continually lengthen to find the one that escaped.
I will wait for you for the last time
at the place
where fragrant resin is diffused from freshly-cut stumps.

A Muffler Named Vladimir

A black rabbit, a curly lie with twinkling red eyes around my neck, warmth as long as northern Europe's winters. *Hello, Vladimir!* The bristly black mustache lying in a tomb at Red Square, fantastically pricking the ribs of fat capitalists. *Hello, Vladimir!* Trees thrusting up like skewers against the backdrop of a pitch-dark stage, waiting for Godot like a wind of red silk the trees will shred. *Hello, Vladimir!* I like your amusing performances of Liszt. A slick, soaked *omija* in my ear where black sugar water flows. *Hi, girls! Hi, boys!* Like the smell of blood from a temple firing into the round muzzle of a black pistol. Vladimir with *A Cloud in Trousers,* also *Hi!* Bang-bang-bang, thirty-six silvery tungsten winters have been delivered to me, too. *Vladimir Vladimir.* A muffler named Vladimir, like a long name falling briefly onto shoulders that scatter like dust. She who was fantastically lovely made it for me with dark red wool yarn.

A Song of Crazy Love

Summer.
After walking onto the worn rose-pattern carpet,
shaking white dust,
beating the transparent heart of rain with a stick,

(describing)
stones
as green
death,
as lollipop
songs,
as holes in cheese,

thrust
your erecting leg into the soft plate of the moon
so that new symbols scurry like rats.

3.
Literary Life

*I have labored carefully, not to mock, lament,
or execrate, human actions but to understand them..*
                                    —Spinoza

The First Poetry Book of May

— To SeungHwan

How beautiful "A," "U," and "G" are.
I finally realize the moon's eyelashes are long

Sitting on the tip of a fallen steeple,
frozen white, in summer shorts,
you call the names of the dead.

Every climax is the end of either left or right,
footsteps heading for flickering blue-black candle flames.

You dictate with misspellings,
the sound of sharpening a pencil is heard, the sound
        of clipping toenails of ice,
or perhaps the sound of falling snow
below the silent barbed-wire entanglements.

Now it is May.
You write the sound of black plastic bags blowing,
the sound of red petals tearing,
the sound of candle wax dripping on pale still faces,
the sound of a slender neck being hanged in the first noose.

You write
it's May, always.

My Mind is Already Packed

From the short grass
in the darkness, basil's green fragrance springs up.

I was sleeping like a log, and my face hit the eggplant-purple, musty-smelling wall. I will dump Nietzsche's complete works on the cold floor of this winter boarding house and next year move to a house with windows opening on an arboretum to meet a boy running out of the house wearing nothing but an aromatic necklace and will then bake warm rye bread for you and ask you to hang a large glittering amethyst of memory from a ceiling stained with the urine of mice. Yellow serifs stud the air beyond the bright window where the warped bookshelf was. There were days when I fell asleep with my cheek on the rug, days when I built this house with books.

Dear Mr. Wittgenstein

This is a night that returns to a more profound abyss after a young artist's forehead is spiked by starlight like a sickle flying after falling out from the long handle of darkness.

Mr. Rodin's workplace is very wide and beautiful.

I stroll through plaster figures waiting for their turns to finish the screams they began earlier, and bronze torsos with no limbs striving to caress eternity; smell the fragrance shed by a well-worn black vinyl record of night air as it spins on a turntable of white lilacs. In a place where the smell of tabloids, the smell of Paris' freshly tarred roads, and the smell of laborers' shabby leather boots mingle noisily, I should write about the reputation of the owner of this place and about the births and deaths of his sculptures. If my writing isn't a pleasant taste on everyone's tongue, it might be difficult for me to remain in Paris. In this quiet and disturbing evening, I was awakened from miscellaneous thoughts by a sudden phone call from your foundation clerk. He told me I would be one of a few writers considered to get a pledge of one thousand golden krone from you, and asked if I received support from any other benefactors. After what seemed an endless hesitation, I informed him of a grant that had been so small and seemed to have happened in Old Testament days. If he had been a little bit stupid, he could have confused my voice with the shaking sound of a rusty chain belonging to a dog with desperate eyes and gray mange spots but, frankly speaking, such gold coins . . . as the person who turns over small stones in front of the house yard and rubs the damp backside of the moon every evening . . . only New Poems and . . . endless and nihilistic allies of Vienna . . . in my vacant heart. However, sir, for the record, I have a wife and a daughter . . .

Respectfully and thankfully . . .
Rainer Maria Ril . . .*

*A letter found in the bundle of receipts from the time Rilke stayed in Rodin's workplace located in Meudon, a suburb of Paris.

A Painting

A man walks on a city street.
A woman covered by an enigma falls asleep in the suburbs.
They've never met
While the woman was running around on the street,
the man was hiding in a blue flask.
When he returned to the underground passage and the fog-filled street,
she was reading books while propped against the library's glass pillar.
The woman underlines NoHae Park and Neruda.
The man recites Jammes and Eliot.

While he masterfully plays the cello in a concert,
she slaps piano keys in a school music room,
outside of which
a small path leads to a forest.

Her name is
the woman who steers the moon from the east.

His name is
the man who rides the sun from the west.

There is a moment when all is painted on a higher plane.
The painting on the right joins the painting on the left.
Other scenes are tidily painted over in black.

Made in the '70s

We can say we write at the risk of our lives,
but no one
points a gun at us.
What a tragedy.
Twirling the world like pink hula hoops around our waists,
we eat,
drink,
wait until we
finally
shoot each other.

Friend

You taught me to use
the scales that weigh stars, time, death
so I can be someone
who paints the invisible weight of a peasant's potatoes and apples.

In the long history of insects and capitalist time,
we belong to a family of insects that gnaws porous caves into iron trees.
Yesterday, I touched a prophecy freshly-fallen from the moon.
Dreams descended from distant cosmos will always have countless holes.

In darkness, how wide would my stride need to be
to burst the luminous orange grains?
Can machinery and freedom mingle like the fragrance of lilacs and roses?
If we open the windows of humanity, do we dare to jump
from such heights?
You taught me how strange questions, fountains of brilliant blood, gush
unceasingly in the boundless desert of answers.

Of course, everything may be interpreted
by the groundwater in my mind,
perhaps once a silent blue river.

You are a casually-tossed stone
making infinite ripples that spread to touch the river's edge.

You are a sharp knife gripped by my hand!
Instead of tall monuments or artists, philosophers, great statesmen,
you, beside me,
a naive Moses, a staff to part red seas,
to drown all soldiers from all times in all their armored confidence.

I believe that. Specks of iron
that frantically chase us through the atmosphere of time scatter
between the magnetic fields of death and life.

I believe that even in my many times of doubt,
I am assured of existence as you stand beside me.
Friend, this is the gift:
I have just revised Descartes' first principle.

An Airplane to the Moon

What kind of propeller should I attach to this song?
Am I twenty years old or ten?

Baby, baby, my baby
the moon calls.

What kind of propeller should I attach to my airplane?
An airplane flying
to a moon like the expression in my mom's eyes.
I want large, hard wings,
a propeller with a deafening roar.

The roaring airplane I painted flies
to the luminous moon I painted.

Inside the picture is silence.
I look into it.
The moon in the picture looks like a man's jaundiced eye;
the airplane has white petal-like propellers.
My sigh creates the wind in the picture.
One, two . . . the petals of the propeller flutter.
I raise my head and cry, *That airplane is flying to the moon.*
The moon pats me
with its long shadowy hand.

Tomorrow paint it again.

Literary Life

The stars are dead. The animals will not look.
We are left alone with . . .
History . . .
— W. H. Auden

They rush us to decide. At least before next spring . . .

For a long time no writer
could write a masterpiece like Goethe,
one great page to encourage young people in yellow vests
to fire their guns at their own temples without hesitation.

They rush us to decide
between red livers swaying on meat hooks, staining the floor,
and dry words
hanging from upside-down brass question marks.

We need an accomplishment comparable to *The Sorrows of Young Werther,*
at least before next spring . . .
Bullets of unemployment
to drive young people to grief; if not death
at least holes shot through temporary workers' orange banners.

Maybe so. For a young person to develop into a great artist,

we may again need
a farmer's cracked forehead, like gashes on a wooden chopping board,
a fisherman's cold mast
scraped from the blue breast of a harbor that reeks of fish,
sweet violence stabbing fat thighs of sorrow!

Bureaucrats rush us to decide.
Do they want to teach us
that songs will surely soar to the sky like jackdaws

carrying the slick intestines of devastation and corruption?
                    Or
haste for free trade and proliferation of wailing and agony?

They rush us to decide.

To raise the price of white pills for tubercular poets;
to feed novelists healthy as Balzac
spotted cows fed on mother cows.

To give our sleeping neighbors the gift of cities where industrial waste
from beautiful countries enters like the Trojan Horse,
a story about toxic chemicals streaming into the ear of the silent noon
as in *Hamlet*.

You guys rush us to decide.

These decisions
shouldn't be made carefully, shouldn't rustle
like grape clusters pulled from paper bags,

but made stealthily,
like a knife that swifty slashes a plastic bag and drops
before the crowd gathers.

Childhood

Time surrounded by high, blue brick walls.
Happy time composed of shining lies.
Winter sun rubbing a rabbit's frozen ears
with its red velvet gloves.

Ice slides down the back of your neck.
Shocked, you become an adult
and open a notebook, groping through the fog.
Raindrops on the dark ink of clumsy sentences.

Despite sable cookies and an arbutus wood bed
miseries can't fall asleep, get caught in a fence of thorns.
Lower back pain slips through moonlit morphine fingers.
You slowly bend at the waist
Cold waves beneath your stomach.

You have drifted away to an unfamiliar shore
where sand is shoveled and midnight oil is burned.

When you awake and open clam shells,
startled childhood eyes prickled by trembling eyelashes
peek at you. Deep red pearls.

Quo Vadis?

Where did the crying kids go?
Even the wind stops.
Twisted string tied our green secrets
in small notebooks
where we wrote numbers for the first time.
Where?

In the cold, the hair of a cat that fell in water is freezing white.

Wooden xylophone,
the sound of evening bells from a distant village.
Where?

The shabby shelf
                The fire at a foreigners' detention center in Yeosu
smelled of paper that had wrapped apples and stars,
                killed ten illegal immigrants and injured seventeen
smelled of paper that had wrapped apples and stars.
                To prevent the detainees' escape
we peeled off and hid thin, crumpled blue candy wrappers
                they waited to open the iron-barred doors
we peeled off and hid thin, crumpled blue candy wrappers
                the immigrants choked to death on fumes.

We moved our tongues along the candy's sweet swirls;
we, young, climbed over the high fence
and fell like raindrops on the neighbor's yard;
red fruit hanging from branches
still follows us.

On a frosted pane of glass, beads of water
stream down clear stains' paths.
In the cold, the smoked hair of a cat
is freezing crisp as new money.

We gather ash grey clouds
that rise like wheat bread.
We tear bread soaked in the blood of the detained
as it gets extremely dark in the evening. Now, to where?

Love Affair

I want to know this kind of love.
A young Mexican man in a white shirt collapsed in the desert
crossing the U.S. border.
I want to marry
you.
I want to go to Baghdad
during the silent time when
green rose
buds burst into bloom
as loudly as bombs
and kiss you
to warm-hearted applause
from the hands of the massacred.

Lying together
in a big transparent drop of water
we will ask
a silver fish passing by,
Why is poetry written even in
a country of genocide?
It is beautiful, but weird.

My Grandmother

was a black chifferobe covered with morning spider webs;
shrank little by little like the Cumaean Sybil;
always wore a large skirt;
was smoothly planed by wind. Her every part grew thin
as a brown piece of paper passing between my clenched knees.

Giggling, she spread her large skirt.
Coral-red chairs carrying lamentation
were connected like third-class seats on a train.
The stink of liquor and urine reeked from
various household items piled like yellow gardenia petals.
The child whose rotting teeth were beginning to lengthen
shrieked and giggled.

Inside one or two drops of liquor
trickled down the wrinkles of her pursed lips,
monsoon seasons set in,
 and several winters passed with gaping mouths,
frozen hearts slowly pushing the ark
overloaded with misery to meet her every moment.

She hung like a thin piece of wet cardboard
on a barrren laurel bough.

Snap! I broke the bough and buried it in the ground.

In the Small Glass Jar with a Yellow Lid

If I could put
a person made of clay
with snowflakes falling on it.

If I could put
the long neck of a faceless woman,
a never-used white smokestack,
the handsome hindquarters of running horses,
a field of green nails.

When I got on the train that was long and tasted
like bile,

the small glass jar with a yellow lid was rolling on the black floor,
discarded by the person who sat there before me.

Where did he get off
after riding in this car
full of songs, the sound of big toes breaking?

Subject

As hovering dust
gives a rushed but polite greeting,
as blue beans falling on a mirror
our attentions scatter,

as fragrances buried in the wind's grave,
as shadows of fingers
try to unwind thread from the spool,

objects remain transparent
as the greenness of olive oil
to blaze some other time,

as the gardener of a thorn yard
where thistles, roses, yellow kumquats periodically grow
touches the names with his blind fingers,
the plants absorb red blood like onionskin paper,
as a cuckoo crying behind black curtains
measures the air's humidity,

moonlit night described in Tibetan,
the world too beautiful to be translated,
as a soaring angel
carries anxious children in its one thousand arms,

as a maze of alleys toward your door,
stairway of silk,
glittering streets tearing apart,
never entering your house

as something
spurting from the ambiguous heart,
someone's thumb pinching and releasing the artery,

stars fall
from the vaulted blue ceiling of a circus tent,

as a boy acrobat letting go
to cross to the other side

may not reach the omnipresent white wrist.

The Beginning of a Certain Song

You gave me cold.
My frozen fingers in your apple green turtleneck
like pussy willows.

You gave me darkness.
My eyes in the glare when the basement light flares on.

Lips were opened to me.
The baffled heat of a stovepipe
connected to the breath of the stove with cedar burning inside.

You gave me money.
The first thing I bought was a pencil and small eraser.

You gave me a knife.
The feeling when I sliced a zucchini and my white wrist for the first time.

You gave me damp bedclothes,
silence drifting with the smell of burgundy ferns;

gave me nothing.
Dead stars.
Time of spores.

And the enigma began.

Page 9: Choi Seung-ja (born 1952) is a well-known Korean poet who often employs radical language and imagery to resist gender discrimination.

Page 16: The poem "Snow Queen" was inspired by the image of the Snow Queen in the fairy tale by Hans Christian Andersen.

Page 18: René Descartes. French: March 31, 1596 – February 11, 1650) was a French philosopher, mathematician, and scientist. Dubbed the father of modern Western philosophy, much of subsequent Western philosophy is a response to his writings.

Page 19: Loaches are various Eurasian and African freshwater fishes of the family *Cobitidae* and related families of the order *Cypriniformes*, having barbels around the mouth.

Page 23: The first sentence is from Charles Baudelaire's "The Possessed," as translated by William Aggeler.

Page 30: This poem was inspired by the popular Japanese animated TV show "Paul in Fantasyland," in which Belt Satan is the demonic ruler.

Page 31: A telos is an ultimate end or purpose, in a fairly-constrained sense used by philosophers such as Aristotle. In contrast to telos, techne is the rational method involved in producing an object or accomplishing a goal or objective.

Page 35: Friedrich Wilhelm Nietzsche (October 15, 1844 – August 25, 1900) was a German philosopher, cultural critic, poet, philologist, and Latin and Greek scholar whose work has exerted a profound influence on Western philosophy and modern intellectual history.

Page 38: The magic square is a square grid (equal number of rows and columns) filled with distinct numbers such that the numbers in each row, and in each column, as well as the numbers in the main and secondary diagonals, all add up to the same value, called the magic constant.

Page 40: Guillaume Apollinaire (French. August 26, 1880 – November 9, 1918) was a French poet, playwright, short story writer, novelist, and art critic of Polish descent. He is considered one of the foremost poets of the early 20th century, as well as one of the most impassioned defenders of Cubism and a forefather of Surrealism.

Page 46: Hide glue is a powder of the connective tissue of animals mixed with warm water and kept warm durng use, allowing repositioning for an extended period. It is used extensively in wood veneering and cabinet making.

Herod (Roman. 74/73 BCE – 4 BCE), also known as Herod the Great and Herod I, appears in the Christian Gospel of Matthew as the ruler of Judea who orders the Massacre of the Innocents at the time of the birth of Jesus.

John was, according to the Christian Gospel of Luke, beheaded AD 29 by Herod Antipas, who imprisoned him in revenge for John's condemnation of his incestuous marriage to his brother's wife, Herodias. Her daughter, Salome, danced for Herod, who rewarded her by offering her whatever she wished. On the advice of her mother, she requested the head of John the Baptist on a platter. Herod was grieved at being requested to execute him, but having given his oath before witnesses, he commanded that it be done

Page 52: The penultimate line, "Fail again, fail better," is a quote from "Westward Ho," in *Nowhere On* (1989) by Samuel Beckett.

Page 56: Godot is the main character in *Waiting for Godot*, a play by Samuel Beckett, in which two characters, Vladimir and Estragon, wait for the arrival of someone named Godot who never arrives.

Omija is the Korean five-flavor berry (*Schisandra chinensis*). It contains five distinct flavors and is frequently used as a health drink.

A Cloud in Trousers is a book-length poem by Vladimir Mayakovsky written in 1914 and first published in 1915. It is considered to be one of the cornerstones of the Russian Futurist poetry.

Page 59: Baruch Spinoza (Dutch; born Benedito de Espinosa, Portuguese: (November 24,1632–February 21, 1677) was a Dutch philosopher who came to be considered one of the great rationalists of 17th-century philosophy. Spinoza's magnum opus, the posthumous *Ethics*, in which he opposed Descartes' mind–body dualism, has earned him recognition as one of Western philosophy's most important thinkers.

Page 61: The Gwangju Massacre occurred from May 18-27, 1980 when Republic of Korea army forces brutally suppressed a pro-democratization movement in the city by shootings, beatings and bayonetings; some estimates put the number of civilian deaths at over 600 (there is no official death toll). The effects of this incident are still being felt today in Korean local and international politics. "A," "U," and "G" are titles of three poems by SeungHwan Song, who was born in Gwangju.

Page 64: NoHae Park is a Korean poet and photographer. His first book, *Dawn of Labor*, was banned in Korea. In 1989, he formed the South Korean Socialist Workers' Alliance, which was taboo at that time. He was arrested in 1991 and sentenced to life in prison. In 1998, he was pardoned by President Kim Daejung.

Page 67: Descartes first principle is: "I think, therefore I am."

Page 69: This poem was written in reference to the dispute over the Free Trade Agreement between South Korea and the United States. The FTA was signed in Spring, 2007.

Johann Wolfgang (von) Goethe. German: (August 28, 1749 – March 22, 1832) was a German writer and statesman. In his famous poem, "Prometheus," the title character is a creative and rebellious spirit who angrily defies God and revolts.

The Sorrows of Young Werther, one of Goethe's most famous novels, is about a young artist of a sensitive and passionate temperament who becomes involved in a love triangle that ultimately leads to his suicide.

A jackdaw is a carrion-eating bird in the crow family.

In Shakespeare's *Hamlet*, Claudius murders the king by pouring poison into his ear. Honoré de Balzac. French: May 20, 1799 – August 18, 1850) was a French novelist and playwright.

Page 71: Sable cookies are a French butter cookie.

Arbutus (madrone) is one of the strongest and most expensive woods in the world.

Page 72: *Quo vadis*, is said in John 16:5 and means *Where are you going?*

Page 75: The Cumaean Sibyl was the priestess presiding over the Apollonian oracle at Cumae, a Greek colony located near Naples, Italy.

The Translators

YoungShil Ji and Daniel T. Parker are a married translation team living in Daegu, South Korea. *We, Day by Day* is their third book published by White Pine Press, following *Wild Apple* by HeeDuk Ra (2015) and *Someone Always in the Corner of My Eye* by BoSeon Shim (2016). Ji graduated with a degree in English Language and Literature from Keimyung University and is a translator specializing in contemporary Korean poetry. Parker is an assistant professor for the English Language and Literature Department at Keimyung University, where he has taught since 2001. He also taught at four universities or colleges in the U.S.A. before coming to South Korea and was a newspaper journalist for thirteen years.

The White Pine Press Korean Voices Series

Nobody Checks the Time When They're Happy
Stories by Eun Heekyung
VOLUME 24   978-1-945680-08-3   174 PAGES $16.00

Wolves
Stories by Jeon Sungtae
Translated by Sora Kim Russell
VOLUME 23   978-1-945680-01-4   192 PAGES $16.00

Someone Always in the Corner of My Eye
Poems by BoSeon Shim
Translated by Daniel Parker and YoungShil Ji
Volume 22   978-935210-90-0   92 pages $16.00

Wild Apple
Poems by HeeDuk Ra
Translated by Daniel Parker and YoungShil Ji
Volume 21   978-1-934210-73-3   90 pages $17.99

Modern Family
A Novel by Cheon Myeong-Kwan
Translated by Kyoung-lee Park
Volume 20   978-1-934210-67-2   180 pages $16.00

I Must Be the Wind
Poems by Moon Chung-hee
Translated by Clare You and Richard Silberg
Volume 19   978-1-935210-60-3   118 pages $16.00

One Day, Then Another
Poems by Kim Kwang-Kyu
Translated by Cho Young-Shil
Volume 18   978-1-935210-54-2   104 pages $16.00

The Depths of a Clam: Selected Poems of Kim Kwang-kyu
Translated by Brother Anthony of Taize
Volume 9   1-893996-43-3   160 pages $16.00

Echoing Song: Contemporary Korean Women Poets
Edited by Peter H. Lee
Volume 8   1-893996-35-2   304 pages $18.00

Among the Flowering Reeds: Classic Korean Poems in Chinese
Edited and translated by Kim Jong-gil
Volume 7   1-893996-54-9   152 pages $16.00

Brother Enemy: Poems of the Korean War
Edited and translated by Suh Ji-moon
Volume 6   1-893996-20-4   176 pages $16.00

Shrapnel and Other Stories
Stories of Dong-ha Lee
Translated by Hyun-jae Yee Sallee
Volume 5   1-893996-53-0   176 pages $16.00

Strong Wind At Mishi Pass
Poems by Tong-gyu Hwang
Translated by Seong-kon Kim & Dennis Maloney
Volume 4   1-893996-10-7   118 pages $15.00

A Sketch of the Fading Sun
Stories of Wan-suh Park
Translated by Hyun-jae Yee Sallee
Volume 3   1-877727-93-8   200 pages $15.00

Heart's Agony: Selected Poems of Chiha Kim
Translated by Won-chun Kim and James Han
Volume 2   1-877727-84-9   128 pages $14.00

The Snowy Road: An Anthology of Korean Fiction

Translated by Hyun-jae Yee Sallee

Volume 1   1-877727-19-9   168 pages $12.00